£4.50

© 1992 GRANDREAMS LIMITED

Written by John Kercher, layout and design by Louise Ivimy and Joanna Winslow.
Photographs supplied by All Action, Retna Pictures Ltd,
Pictorial Press Ltd.

Published by
GRANDREAMS LIMITED
Jadwin House
205/211 Kentish Town Road
London
NW5 2JU

Printed in Belgium

ISBN 0 86227 962 3

CONTENTS

Robert Thorne Clarke

The Michael Ja

Michael has come a long way since the days of singing country and western songs beside his mum's piano in Indiana. Here's the Jackson guide to becoming a pop legend....

When Michael Jackson first burst onto the music scene with his brothers in *The Jackson 5* it was easy to see that the little ten-year-old boy who fronted the group as lead singer was something special.

His vocal talents and expertise on the dance floor were obvious and he began working as the choreographer for the group when he was just eleven. He had a professional maturity that was way beyond his years, but even then no-one imagined just what a giant he would become in the pop world.

Michael was born on 29th August 1958 to Joseph and Katherine Jackson in the town of Gary, Indiana. Right from the beginning, the sound of music filled their house as Joseph Jackson played semi-professionally with a band called *The Falcons*.

There was also a lot of singing in the Jackson household,

especially as his mother was a good pianist and used to accompany the vocal sessions.

Surprisingly, even with so much talent available, Michael and his brothers did not have any

immediate inclination to enter the music business. It would be a tough time trying to break into it and besides they were into too many other things like playing games and watching television.

According to Michael's mother it was only when the television broke down that they found themselves with nothing to do and, to alleviate the boredom, they formed an impromptu band.

It was not so much pop music that occupied their singing sessions but country and western. It isn't the kind of music you would associate with Michael but his mother knew a lot of those tunes and they would sing along with her as she played.

Gradually the boys began to develop their own unique style, copying and practising other artists material with their own arrangements. They were

quite raw at the beginning but they found it was a lot of fun and, slowly, their father began to realise what a talented bunch of kids he had.

Michael's musical tastes included *The Supremes* fronted by Diana Ross who were part of the Motown Sound and *The Temptations*. He was obviously influenced by their slick and intricate dance routines.

Over a period of years, Michael and his brothers developed an act doing cover versions

career she approached the boss of her record company, Motown, to see if he would be prepared to give them a hearing.

Motown had already established itself as one of the major labels in the world with a string of hit records and important bands and artists. So a chance like this was not to be missed.

Michael and his brothers were already hardened to life on the road and they had performed in New York before performing for Motown Records. But even with this under their belt, nothing prepared them for the splendour of Berry Gordy's (Motown's manager) home in Detroit.

"It was unbelievable," says Michael's brother, Jermaine. "Like nothing we'd seen before. Barry had his own golf course and even a bowling alley in the basement."

For Michael and his brothers it was like a giant playground. But despite being in awe of the affluence surrounding them they auditioned well and Berry Gordy was suitably impressed.

It was 1969 when Michael and the group

mixed in with their own songs. When they began playing at local events they were an instant success, particularly Michael whose talent for putting across a song was obvious to anyone who watched him perform.

The word 'perform' was significant. Whilst other kids of his age would sing a song, Michael would perform it like a real artist.

One of the first people to talent spot *The Jackson 5* was Diana Ross. She approached Michael and his brothers and said that she liked their act and thought they had a promising future in music. After establishing that the Jacksons were interested in a recording

signed their first recording contract and got their first number one hit with *I Want You Back*. They were the talk of the business and were soon appearing on national television.

he and his brothers were still forming their act, and the huge success of his debut single meant that he became a school personality and even his own classmates wanted his autograph.

appeared. Michael wasn't too happy about having to study - every morning he had to sit in his hotel suite and do maths, English and geography. Looking back he doesn't regret it - the maths have served him well, as he is now an astute businessman.

Michael went to live with Diana Ross at her home for a while and it's fair to say that she was instrumental in helping him project his stage presence. She was already an established and seasoned performer and provided him with lots of valuable tips.

When Michael came to Britain with *The Jackson 5* in the 1970s the scenes were incredible. Thousands of fans waited at the airport for him and there was one dramatic incident in which a bunch of fans broke through a police cordon. For a moment it looked as if Michael would be mobbed, but he managed to run fast enough to elude the crowd. He was unnerved by the experience and realised that being a star wasn't easy.

It is hard to believe that Michael ever attended school since he seems to have been in the recording business for ever. But he started out just like any other kid. He was still at school when

But you can't stay at school for long when you suddenly have a million selling hit record. So Michael was assigned a private tutor who went along with him and the group wherever they

Since then few fans have managed to get that close. Michael isn't quite the hermit he has been made out to be

of the movies and an admirer of the classic *Wizard Of Oz* and so the prospect of remaking the film with an all black cast appealed to him enormously.

He took on the role of the scarecrow and Diana Ross filled the part of Dorothy, originally played by Judy Garland.

It was an ambitious project which could have made Michael into a movie star as well as a pop star. But although it was entertaining, the film was not a box office hit.

Michael's next career move came as a result of meeting Quincy Jones. Quincy had been a long time in the music business as an established jazz musician and then producer. His meeting with Michael was to spark off a legendary partnership, similar to that between George Martin and the

- he is quite happy to stand before his fans, but now it's at a much safer distance.

Between 1969 and 1971, Michael and the group had four number one hit singles. Many more followed, until in 1976, the group decided to change their record label. It was a difficult moment, because brother, Jermaine, wanted to stay with Motown.

It seemed more and more obvious that Michael would gradually become a solo artist as he dominated the recordings and always seemed to be the centre of attention.

Then Michael made an excursion into the world of film. He had always been a great fan

Beatles. He was an arranger and producer admired throughout the pop world.

When they went into the studio to record Michael's first solo album, *Off The Wall*, the result was an incredible piece of production which went

shooting up the charts and demonstrated that Michael was a performer and artist in his own right.

But this was only the start. If everyone was astounded by the success of *Off The Wall* they hadn't reckoned on *Thriller*, which was to follow.

In between the albums Michael embarked on a tour with his brothers. They had not been enjoying the phenomenal success that he had but Michael's presence on stage lifted the whole group. Michael even spent a lot of time working out the designs and ideas for the elaborate stage sets that were used on the tour.

When *Thriller* finally emerged from the secrecy that surrounded it, people knew that pop history was in the making. Steven Spielberg was brought in to direct the dramatic video for the title track, and sales of the album topped forty-five million copies making it the greatest selling album of all time.

Then Michael went into slow motion. He spent ages working on ideas for his next album and the end product was *Bad*. Michael emerged from hibernation with a new look. He appeared dressed in leather and silver chains, as though he was trying to shake off an image that had been too clean.

Then the same thing happened again. After all the hype had faded and *Bad* had slipped from the charts, Michael went back into musical retirement. *Dangerous* was eventually released after umpteen postponements to make alterations, but the magic was still there - it went straight to the top of the charts.

Michael will be showcasing his talents on stage again for certain and it's rumoured that he might be making more films. Whatever he does you can be sure that it will be in his usual inimitable style!

in
Disguise

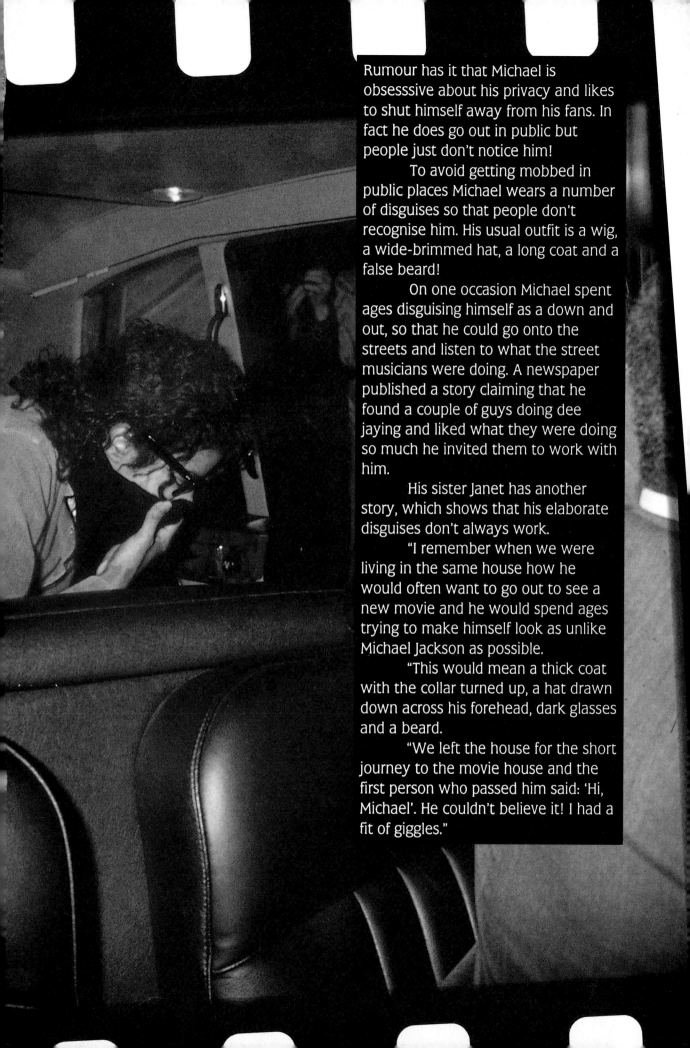

Rumour has it that Michael is obsesssive about his privacy and likes to shut himself away from his fans. In fact he does go out in public but people just don't notice him!

To avoid getting mobbed in public places Michael wears a number of disguises so that people don't recognise him. His usual outfit is a wig, a wide-brimmed hat, a long coat and a false beard!

On one occasion Michael spent ages disguising himself as a down and out, so that he could go onto the streets and listen to what the street musicians were doing. A newspaper published a story claiming that he found a couple of guys doing dee jaying and liked what they were doing so much he invited them to work with him.

His sister Janet has another story, which shows that his elaborate disguises don't always work.

"I remember when we were living in the same house how he would often want to go out to see a new movie and he would spend ages trying to make himself look as unlike Michael Jackson as possible.

"This would mean a thick coat with the collar turned up, a hat drawn down across his forehead, dark glasses and a beard.

"We left the house for the short journey to the movie house and the first person who passed him said: 'Hi, Michael'. He couldn't believe it! I had a fit of giggles."

BLACK, WHITE AND DANGEROUS

Michael Jackson never does things by halves. When he put his ideas forward for the special effects in the *Black or White* video the director nearly keeled over backwards. For money to Michael, who has an estimated fortune of £25 million, means little. He just thinks in terms of what is going to look good on screen.

Eventually, his ideas were tailored to fit a 'realistic' budget of four million dollars. For a video lasting eleven minutes that's pretty hefty by anyone's standards.

Michael's dream is to exceed the 45 million sales of the *Thriller* album, but just what he had planned for *Dangerous*, no-one knew.

When *Black or White* was shown, people wondered why it cost so much money. It is a strange hotch potch of sequences, the best of which shows faces from every race appear in serial, each one melting into the next. As well as being a wacky feat of photography it also conveyed that whatever colour skin we have, we all belong to one race.

The strangest section of the video is when Michael turns into a panther, prowls about a bit and then turns back into himself and does a mean dance routine involving a lot of window smashing and loud foot tapping. People speculated about the relevance of this to the rest of the video, but in the end put it down to Michael's quirky creativity.

The video also ended the speculation that Michael had decided to change his image. Madonna had been trying to persuade him to adopt a new look and it was said that she told him his military-style jackets and long hair were old fashioned. If anyone knows about new images then it is Madonna who has gone through more changes than a chameleon.

Would Michael crop the locks? Pictures of him with a sleek short style appeared, but Michael was playing a joke on his fans. He had swept his long hair to one side and had a profile shot done to give the impression of a new look.

But he was just the same, and many of

his fans were relieved. He still wears a soft hat pushed forward on his face as he dances and he seems determined to keep those military jackets!

Black or White did make a concession to rap music though. Michael had always said that he would never use rap on his records, but using it

has given the album a nineties flavour.

The album *Dangerous* took three years to put together and Michael risked some of the material sounding dated. But then he has always done things his way, irrespective of current trends and it has worked for him up till now.

FACTS

It's said that Michael wanted to get experts to teach his chimpanzee Bubbles to talk, so that he could communicate with him better. This isn't as crazy as it sounds - some chimps in America can learn several dozen words in sign language.

Michael was also warned against keeping a chimp as a pet as they can become violent in their old age and attack people.

Hammer, formerly known as MC Hammer, calls Michael 'The Glove', because of the single glove that he wears.

On one of Michael's world tours he wanted the most spectacular stage effects possible and came up with the idea of making the front two rows of the audience disappear and reappear.

But it was considered too difficult to achieve. However a British magician said that he could have done it quite easily.

Michael fasts for one day of every week to rid his body of toxins. It's not so weird as it sounds - Larry Hagman (alias JR in *Dallas*) does the same.

Michael loves Disneyland so much that he is said to have a permanent hotel suite reserved for him there.

He used to be a great fan of the bizarre rock star, Alice Cooper.

It's rumoured in the music business that Michael's recent recording, film and merchandising contract is worth more than one billion dollars!

Michael confesses that one of his favourite hobbies is daydreaming.

People visiting Michael's house are requested to sign papers saying they won't talk about his home or what they discussed.

Quincy Jones' nickname for Michael is Smelly because he says he has a good nose for a hit.

Michael's favourite all-time film is *E.T.* Why? Because he reminds Michael of himself!

The *Jackson 5* used to be so popular they had an animated TV series made about them.

One of Michael's best friends is Paul McCartney. Their very first musical collaboration was *Girlfriend* from *Off The Wall*.

Michael is fascinated by the Elephant Man and it's said that he even tried to buy his skeleton from a hospital. The

designed by Hollywood's Bill Whitten. It takes a seamstress nearly 40 hours of embroidery to complete just one.

When Michael went on his 1987 *Bad* tour 794,000 people in the UK saw him perform live. They paid just under a total of £13 million.

The album *Ben*, which was released in 1972, had pictures of rats on the cover. It was withdrawn!

Michael is reputed to take a bath in mineral water. The reason being that it has less pollutants in it than ordinary tap water.

Alexander O' Neal once said of Michael Jackson: "He's a great singer but he's not the most masculine guy in the world is he?"

hospital said that it wasn't for sale.

His favourite item of clothing is a pair of steel-toed Mexican cowboy boots.

Michael is a vegan and likes nothing better than knocking back a glass or two of carrot juice. When he first went vegetarian he lost 25 lbs.

Michael's famous gloves are

Michael behind

the scenes

THE
RECORDS

ichael's recording career began in a way that other stars can only dream of - four number one hit singles one after the other.

Soon after signing with Motown Records, Michael and his brothers stormed into the charts with *I Want You Back* which gave their fans a taste of what was to come. They didn't have to wait long as the now established classic, *ABC* charted soon after. Despite the fact that Michael's high voice was obviously that of a youngster, there was a maturity which few kids of his age could manage. Not to mention the way he performed it.

and *The Best of Michael Jackson*

And the *The Jackson 5* also continued to churn out hit albums. There was *I Want You Back, ABC, Third Album, Going Back To Indiana, Get It Together, Dancing Machine* and *Moving Violation.*

It was the year of 1979 that proved to be a landmark for Michael when, teaming up with producer and arranger Quincy Jones, he released *Off The Wall.* This was the start of the true Michael Jackson legend. Four singles from the album became hits in their own right: *Don't Stop Till You Get Enough, Rock With You, Off The Wall*

The next couple of singles were *The Love That You Save* and *I'll Be There.* The dollars started rolling in and it seemed that Michael and the group could do no wrong.

Then Michael embarked on a solo career and started producing hits such as *Got To Be There, I Wanna Be Where You Are, Rockin' Robin* and several albums, including *Got To Be There, Music and Me, Forever, Michael*

and *She's Out Of My Life.* The album sales topped eight million.

Michael still collaborated with *The Jacksons* (no longer *The Jackson 5* since the departure of Jermaine) and helped to make *Lovely One, Heartbreak Hotel* and *Can You Feel It* monster hits in the early eighties.

Then came *Thriller* - the album that was to change Michael from a star into a megastar and the greatest

recording artist that the world has ever seen. The album was a work of genius - the hit singles poured from it into the charts as if there was an unstoppable flow. They included *The Girl Is Mine, Wanna Be Starting Something, Billie*

Jean, Thriller, Beat It, The Lady In My Life, and *Baby Be Mine.*

Despite all the awards that *Thriller* received (the video is still the best seller of all time) Michael claimed that he still wasn't satisfied. He was delighted with the forty-five million sales figure but he believed he could do better.

But when *Bad* was released Michael's dream failed to materialise. It sold 25 million copies but didn't collect any awards.

The hit singles from the album compensated somewhat. *Bad*, the title track, was the first to make it into the charts and that was followed by *The Way You Make Me Feel, Man In The Mirror, I Just Can't Stop Loving You, Dirty Diana* and *Smooth Criminal.* Michael had done it again with the help of Quincy Jones.

The pressure was certainly on Michael to come up with something comparable for his next album and it turned out to be three years in the making.

He decided to do *Dangerous* without the help of Quincy Jones, a tremendous gamble because Quincy had been a major influence on the success of *Off The Wall, Thriller* and *Bad.* It seemed that Michael was contemplating a new direction. As it transpired, *Dangerous* wasn't radically different from Michael's previous records.

The cover of the album featured a dramatic picture of Michael's eyes. Chimpanzees and other animals feature strongly on the cover and if you look carefully you can see Michael at different points of his career worked into the elaborate friezes.

The number seven is also

cryptically featured in several places, perhaps because there are seven tracks on each double album. A nuclear disarmament symbol appears on one of the columns showing Michael's feelings on the subject of war and there are also references to the artist Botticelli.

The hype that preceded the album's release paid off - fans awaited it eagerly and the first single to be released from it went straight to number one. But Michael won't be satisfied until he has managed to produce an album that outsells *Thriller*.

Janet on Michael

When Michael was living in his first mansion, his sister, Janet, was staying with him and had a unique picture of how he worked.

"He was such a tough taskmaster for himself," she says. Michael would just disappear into the recording studio that he had in the house and spend all day working out ideas for new material for his albums.

"And as for the dancing, you couldn't get him off his feet. He would work out routines in front of mirrors for hours, trying to perfect new steps that he would use in his videos and on stage. He has so much incredible energy."

In fact Janet says that it was Michael who persuaded her to do more recording herself.

"He would often call me into his studio when he wanted me to work on some ideas that he had, and I would sing with him. Then one day he told me that I really ought to try and make it on my own in the business. Until then I had always been a bit hesitant, but I decided to give it a try."

Michael's advice was spot on, as Janet went on to become one of the top recording artists in the world!

FAMOUS FRIENDS

One of the best things about being as famous as Michael Jackson is that you get to meet lots of other famous people too! And if there's someone who you haven't met but would like to, then you just pick up the phone. Here's Michael with some of his Hollywood mates...

MAD MICHAEL

Janet Jackson once said of Michael that he sometimes "loses touch with reality," and if you believe what the papers say he's a pretty eccentric guy. Here are his top ten maddest moments...

Michael eats flowers! He was staying in a hotel in Florida in 1988 and ate nothing but roses, carnations and the like. "We were ordering about £30 of flowers every day," says the hotel manager. "When Michael left there were empty flower vases everywhere."

He sleeps in an oxygen tank! Except he doesn't really. The truth behind this claim is that Michael was visiting some kids in hospital and he climbed in to an oxygen to "see what it was like". He said at the time, "I could live 150 years in this."

On February 15 1992 Michael became an African King. He became honarary monarch of the Ivory Coast's Agni tribe and received a gold chain, a loincloth and a crown during the ritual.

When Michael found out that one of the chimps in his zoo was having a baby he hired an architect to build a nursery for it!

Michael owns a briefcase with a hidden tape recorder inside, and six telephone scrambling devices (so no-one can listen into his calls).

On September 14 1990 Michael was awarded the "Michael Jackson Good Scout Humanitarian Award" by the LA Boy Scouts of America.

Michael's boa constrictor came in pretty handy for Paula Abdul. She was looking after it when a burglar broke into her house. The burglar took one look at Muscles slithering in his direction and changed his mind!

Michael wore a spooky werewolf mask in his *Thriller* video and then sold it at Phillips auction rooms on April 24th. The starting price was £1,500.

When Michael's pet pig, Jasmine started to batter down walls and doors in his house he called in a pet psychologist to psychoanalyse her.

When Michael received an Entertainer Of The Nineties award from President George Bush of America he didn't say a word to him. Then as he was leaving he lowered the window of his limosine and whispered, "Hi, I love you," to the crowd.

THE HOUSE THAT MICHAEL BUILT

Michael lives in a place called Neverland Valley. It's a complex of houses and grounds built in Swiss chalet style and it includes a private zoo, a 100 seater cinema, amusement arcades, a library, a music room and, of course, Michael's own luxury apartment.

Neverland Valley is shrouded in mystery, mainly because no-one is ever allowed to go there. Until recently no journalists have set foot in the place and it is heavily guarded twenty-four hours a day, seven days a week.

The entrance to Neverland Valley is noticeably understated, the driveway could be anyone's. It's only when you catch sight of the statues lining the drive - bronze statues of characters from Peter Pan - that you realise you're somewhere extraordinary.

The whole estate is based on the theme of Peter Pan's Never Never land where children never grow up. As well as amusement arcades Michael has a museum full of his own memorabilia - sequinned gloves, jackets from previous tours and the car and the robot from the Moonwalker film, to name a few.

The cinema is pretty removed from reality as well. Along the sides are huge animated puppets in boxes - all you have to do is press a button and they start moving. In typical self-indulgent style there is one of Michael doing the Moonwalk. The cinema even has its own bedrooms so that if Michael or his guests are too sleepy after a film to go back to their rooms they can simply crash out where they are.

This isn't *quite* as lazy as it sounds. Getting from one place to another in Neverland Valley can be quite time-consuming because it's so large. Michael gets about in a jeep.

If you're lucky enough to be a guest of Michael's you'll have your own separate self-contained apartment. (Unless your name is Elizabeth Taylor, in which case you'll stay in the main house.) You will be able to spend your time playing games and records in the amusement arcades (all free of course), visiting the llamas, chimps and giraffes in the zoo, browsing through the museum or eating meals prepared by Michael's personal chefs.

FAMILY MATTERS

A 2 Z

A is for Paula Abdul who has helped choreograph some of Michael's famous dance routines.

B is for Bubbles, Michael's pet chimpanzee.

C is for for cash! He is rumoured to be worth a phenomenal $350 million.

D is for for singer, Diana Ross, who brought Michael and his brothers to Motown Records at the beginning of their music career.

E is for eternal youth.

F is for friends. Michael's mates include Jane Fonda, Brooke Shields, Elizabeth Taylor and the star of *Home Alone*, Macaulay Culkin.

G is for glove, Michael's trademark.

H is for Hollywood Walk Of Fame, where Michael has his name on a star.

I is for instrument. He first started out learning to play the drums.

J is for Janet Jackson, his sister.

K is for kid. Michael is said to hate the idea of growing up.

L is for Louis the llama. Another one of Michael's freaky pets.

M is for Michael's famous Moonwalk on stage and video.

N is for nose. Did he or didn't he?

O is for *Off The Wall*, Michael's best selling album.

P is for Peter Pan, Michael's favourite fictional character.

Q is for Quincy Jones who has produced three of Michael's albums.

R is for ranch. Michael's covers 2,500 acres in California.

S is for Steven Spielberg, the director of *ET* and the *Thriller* video. Also a good friend of Michael's.

T is for *Thriller*, the greatest selling album ever.

U is for uniform. Michael's very partial to military style jackets.

V is for video. His have become classics.

W is for waxworks. When Michael had his done for Madame Tussauds in London, he flew over to see it.

X is for his exciting stage shows.

Y is for you, the fans.

Z is for zoo. Michael has an incredible assortment of animals on his ranch.